Mathematical Journeys

Departure Points

Published in January 2007 by ATM

Association of Teachers of Mathematics
7, Shaftesbury Street, Derby DE23 8YB
Telephone 01332 346599
Fax 01332 204357
e-mail admin@atm.org.uk

Copyright © 2007 by Association of Teachers of Mathematics
All rights reserved
Printed in England

ISBN 978-1-898611-47-9

Further copies may be purchased from the above address

www.atm.org.uk

Contents

1. Routes.................... 1
2. Number Pairs 2
3. Lines and Squares 2
4. Multiplication Square 2
5. Fault Lines 3
6. Sweets 3
7. Discs..................... 4
8. Trihex.................... 4
9. Watch Out 5
10. Bracelets 5
11. Cube Moves 6
12. 1089 6
13. Folds.................... 7
14. Chessboard............... 7
15. Dissections............... 8
16. Cube Nets................ 8
17. Reptiles................... 9
18. Palindromes 10
19. Sixes..................... 10
20. Chains....................11
21. Braille....................11
22. Hexa Puzzles 12
23. Max Box 13
24. Marks on a Ruler 13
25. Jugs 14
26. Painted Cubes............. 14
27. Divisibility 14
28. Consecutive Sums 15
29. Diagonals 15
30. Four Fours 15
31. Arithmogons.............. 16
32. Worms 17
33. Happy Numbers 18
34. Picking Stones 19
35. Magic Shapes............. 19
36. Rectangle Areas........... 20
37. Halving the Board 20
38. Number Cells 21
39. Taking Counters........... 21
40. Two-piece Tangrams 22
41. Lines and Regions......... 22
42. Patio Tiles............... 23
43. Near to the Root 23
44. Calendars 24
45. Quadrant tiles 24
46. Dotty shapes 25
47. Polygons within polygons ... 25
48. Hiccup numbers.......... 25
49. Stamps 26
50. Maximum Area........... 26
51. Breaking Sticks 26
52. Moving arrowheads 27
53. Finding triangles 27
54. Bell ringing 27
55. Elephant walk............ 28
56. Frogs................... 29
57. Round and Round 29
58. All the Digits 30
59. Quotient................ 30
60. Egyptian Fractions......... 31
61. Frog Hopping 32
62. Fleas................... 33
63. Garden Path 34
64. Super-dot Polygons 35
65. The Tethered Goat 36

Mathematical Journeys – Departure Points

Introduction

In 1977 six sessions at the ATM Conference in Nottingham were devoted to activities which would provide pupils with the opportunity to explore and investigate potentially rich mathematical situations. At that time the teachers expressed the opinion that it was not very easy to find sources of suitable starting points for investigations.

The outcome was a pamphlet entitled Points of Departure 1 and it was followed by three more collections of open-ended starting points which have stood the test of time. The investigations in the books were contributed by teachers and they aim to provide interesting ideas for a wide range of interests and ability levels. It is acknowledged by the teachers who contributed to the publications that the investigations are not original. However, they do provide a very rich and interesting resource bank of ideas which are just as valuable for classroom use as they were thirty years ago.

The original books state that although the activities can be given to pupils as they stand, this is not the main intention. The idea is that teachers should adapt the ideas and put them into an appropriate format for their pupils. The amount of structure that teachers might impose is up to the individual.

The strength of the activities is that they allow opportunities for pupils to make choices about the mathematics and equipment they will use and how to record the results. This opportunity to make choices is fundamental to the using and applying element of the National Curriculum.

Although Points of Departure have been amongst ATM's best sellers the Publications Group decided that a change from the original format was needed. We have used a selection of the most popular activities and given the books a new title. We hope you will enjoy trying them again with your pupils.

Mathematical Journeys

1. Routes

a) Start at A and travel along lines only in these two directions → and ↑.

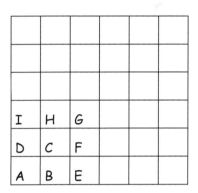

In how many ways can you get from A to each of the lettered points? Try other points. Can you spot some patterns? Can you generalise them?
Can you explain or prove them?

b) Start at A and move in any of these directions →, ↖ and ↗.

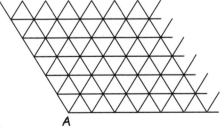

Investigate as before.

c) Invent your own grids and rules for moves.

1

Mathematical Journeys

2. Number Pairs

Choose any number, eg 21.
Form a number pair by taking 21 mod 2, which is 1, and 21 mod 3, which is 0.
So 21 → (1,0). Also 17 → (1,2).
Find all possible such pairs.
Investigate what happens to the pairs when you add, subtract, multiply or divide the original numbers.
Extend this to number triples, etc.

3. Lines and Squares

Here there are 10 straight
lines and 17 squares.

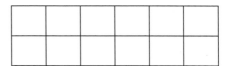

Here there are 9 straight
lines and 20 squares.

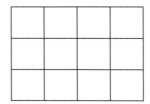

Find the smallest number of lines needed to make exactly 100 squares.
Investigate further.
How many different ways can you make a particular number of squares?

4. Multiplication Square

Make a ten-by-ten multiplication square. Investigate the number patterns.

Mathematical Journeys

5. Fault Lines

Here is a rectangle made with some dominoes.

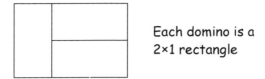

Each domino is a 2×1 rectangle

A fault line is a straight line joining opposite sides of the rectangle. These two rectangles both have one fault line.

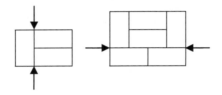

What is the smallest fault free rectangle that you can find?
What is the smallest fault-free square?
Suppose you use 3×1 rectangles instead of dominoes?

6. Sweets

When a boy counted his sweets in piles of four, he had two left over. When he counted them in piles of five, he had one left over. How many sweets could he have had?
Investigate other situations of this type.

7. Discs

a) Here are three circular cardboard discs.
A number is written on the top of each disc.

There is also a number (not necessarily the same) written on the reverse side of each disc.
Throwing the discs in the air, and then adding the numbers on the faces, I have produced the following eight totals:
　　　　　　15, 16, 17, 18, 20, 21, 22, 23.
Can you work out what numbers are written on the reverse side of each disc?

b) Investigate totals produced by discs numbered differently. Can you produce eight consecutive numbers as totals?

Investigate for 2 discs.
Are there ways of numbering 3 discs so each combination gives a different total?

8. Trihex

There are 9 cells on this board, joined by lines.
Each player has 5 counters (one player has red, the other blue).
They take it in turns to put a counter in a cell.
The first player to have three counters in a straight line wins.

Investigate this game.

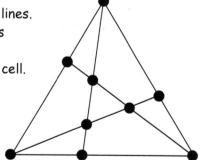

Mathematical Journeys

9. Watch Out

Imagine a city whose streets form a square grid, the sides of each square being 100 metres long, like this:

New York City on
Manhattan Island is
rather like this

Suppose that a policeman is standing at a street corner and that he can spot a suspicious person at 100m. So he can survey a maximum of 400m of street length, like this.

If we have a single block, with 4 corners, we need two policemen.

Two blocks in a row will need 3 policemen.

How many policemen are needed for 3 blocks? 4 blocks? 5 blocks?
What about blocks in squares? In rectangles?
Investigate further and see if you can find some rules.

10. Bracelets

Start with any two numbers less than 10 – say 1 and 5. Make a bracelet of numbers like this:

$$1 \to 5 \to 6 \to 1 \to 7 \to 8 \to 5 \to$$

Can you see how the chain is made?
Continue the chain – what happens?
Choose some more starting numbers and investigate what happens.
How many different chains can you make?
What happens if you use numbers in other bases?

11. Cube Moves

Suppose you have 8 cubes placed on a 3×3 board as shown.

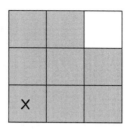

By sliding one cube at a time transfer the cube marked X to the top right-hand corner. How many moves are required?
Which is the best (shortest) route?
How many moves do you need if you are allowed to move more than one cube at a time?
Investigate for boards of different sizes.
What rules?

12. 1089

Write down a 3-digit number, say	742
Reverse the digits	247
Subtract	495
Reverse the digits	594
Add	1089

Do you always get 1089?

What happens if you start with 564?
Can you prove that you will always get 1089?
Are there similar results with 2 digits?
Are there similar results with 4 digits?
Extend to other bases.

Mathematical Journeys

13. Folds

Fold a piece of paper in half, then in half again and then open it out.

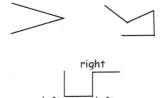

Investigate the shapes produced and the patterns of left and right turns.

14. Chessboard

How many squares here?

Five! Where are they?

How many squares on a 3×3 board?
How many squares on a 4×4 board?
So how many squares are there on a chessboard?

What about other rectangular boards?

How many squares here?

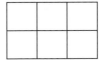

Can you generalise your results?
How many squares on an m × m board?
How many squares on an m × n board?

How many rectangles on any of the boards?

Mathematical Journeys

15. Dissections

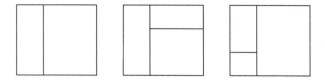

The diagrams show dissections of a 3×3 square into rectangles. The rules are:
1. In each dissection the rectangles are all different.
2. The edges are all integers.

Investigate.

16. Cube Nets

This diagram shows one possible net for a cube.
How many different cube nets can you find?
What about nets for other solids?

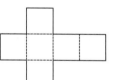

8

17. Reptiles

Squares can be fitted together to make larger similar shapes:

So can these:

And these:

These shapes are called reptiles.
What others can you find?

Mathematical Journeys

18. Palindromes

a) Choose any number, reverse the digits and add:

```
  2 1 6
  6 1 2
  -----
  8 2 8
```

828 is a palindromic number (the same backwards as forwards)

Try another number - reverse and add:

```
  1 5 4
  4 5 1
  -----
  6 0 5
```

605 is not a palindromic number, so we repeat the process:

```
  6 0 5
  5 0 6
  -----
1 1 1 1
```

1111 is palindromic. Does this always happen? Investigate.

b) Are palindromic numbers multiples of 11?

c) The palindromic number 828 is the sum of 216 and its reverse 612. Take some palindromic numbers. Can you always make them by adding a number and its reverse? When you can, are there rules to find the numbers?

19. Sixes

What sums can you find with answer six?

20. Chains

$$6 \to 3 \to 10 \to 5 \to 16 \to ....$$

Rules:
1) If a number is <u>even</u>, divide it by 2
2) If a number is <u>odd</u>, multiply it by 3 and add 1

Continue the chain above. What happens?

Choose other starting numbers and see what happens.
Try to put all your results together on one diagram.

Try changing the rules, e.g. alter rule 2
If a number is <u>odd</u>, multiply it by 3 and subtract 1

21. Braille

Louis Braille, a Frenchman living in the 19th century, invented an alphabet for use by blind people.

The alphabet consisted of raised dots in rectangular patterns. Each pattern of dots was based on a 3 x 2 rectangle.

Here are some of the patterns that were used:

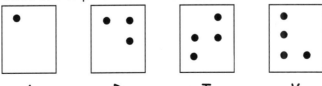

    A   D   T   V

How many different patterns can be made using this system?
Investigate for different sized rectangles.

Mathematical Journeys

22. Hexa Puzzles

Here are four ways of cutting up a hexagon to make further hexagons, parallelograms, equilateral triangles etc.

Investigate ways of dissecting hexagons

Mathematical Journeys

23. Max Box

Suppose you have a square sheet of card measuring 15 cm by 15 cm and you want to use it to make an open box.

You could do this by cutting squares out at the corners and then folding up the sides.

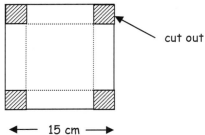

cut out

15 cm

Suppose you want the box to have the maximum possible volume. What size corners would you cut out?

24. Marks on a Ruler

I have a straight edge I want to use as a ruler that will measure any length from 1 cm to 6 cm. I can do this by putting 7 marks on the straight edge in the usual way, but it can be done with fewer, as each mark can be used for different lengths.

With 3 marks

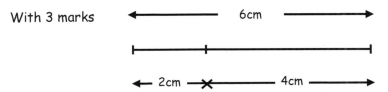

What is the least number of marks I need for all lengths from 1 cm to 6 cm?
Investigate for different lengths. 6

25. Jugs

If you had a 3-litre jug and a 5-litre jug, how could you use them to measure 4 litres? Investigate other problems like this.

26. Painted Cubes

A 3 x 3 x 3 cube is made out of white blocks.

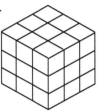

The outside is painted red.
How many little blocks have 3 sides painted? 2 sides? 1 side? 0 sides?
Investigate this for different sizes of cubes.

27. Divisibility

A test to see if a number is divisible by 3 is to add the digits together and if the answer is divisible by 3, so is the original number.

Find divisibility tests for other numbers.
Find divisibility tests for different bases

28. Consecutive Sums

15 = 7 + 8
9 = 2 + 3 + 4 or 4 + 5
10 = 1 + 2 + 3 + 4

These three numbers can be written as the sum of two or more consecutive integers. Are there numbers which cannot be written like this?

Starting with any number, say 42, can you decide whether and how it can be written in this way?

Which numbers, like 9 above, can be split up in more than one way?

29. Diagonals

Investigate the number of squares out by the diagonal of a rectangle (in this diagram it is six).

30. Four Fours

What numbers can you make using four 4's and mathematical symbols?

For example $\dfrac{4}{4} + \dfrac{4}{4} = 2$

$4 + 4 + \dfrac{4}{\sqrt{4}} = 10$

Mathematical Journeys

31. Arithmogons

In an arithmogon, the number in a square must be the sum of the numbers on each side of it:

Solve these if possible:

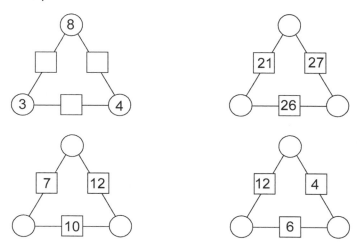

Find a way of solving these (apart from trial and error).
Is there always an answer?
Is there only one answer? When are fractions needed?
When are negative numbers needed?

Try these:

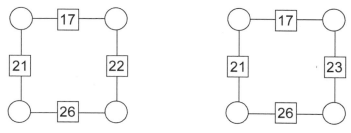

Why not try pentagons? Or hexagons?

16

Mathematical Journeys

32. Worms

Worms leave tracks in layers of mud.

A worm forms a piece of track, turns through 90° forms another piece, turns, forms another piece, turns . . .

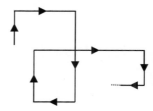

The drawing shows a 1, 2, 3 worm; it makes one unit of track, turns, makes two units of track, turns, makes three units of track, turns, makes one unit of track....

Investigate worms.

Mathematical Journeys

33. Happy Numbers

23 is happy!
Because

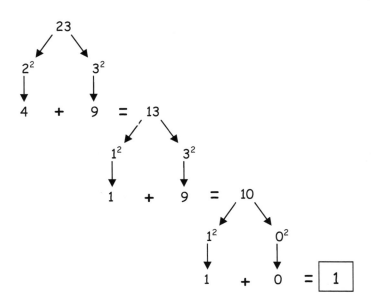

If you end up with a 1, the number you started with is happy.
Is 15 happy?
What about 7? . . . or 24?
Try some others.

How many numbers less than 50 are happy?
Is there a quick way of telling if a number is happy?
Invent a method of producing SAD numbers.
Find out which numbers are SAD using your method.

Mathematical Journeys

34. Picking Stones

This is an old Chinese game, for two players. They take it in turns to select stones from two piles, by taking
either:
at least one stone from one of the piles (all of them if you like),
or:
the same number (at least one) of stones from each pile
The player who takes all the stones on his turn is the winner.

Investigate for different number of stones.

35. Magic Shapes

For the magic square you can put the numbers from 1 to 9 in the spaces so that each unit adds up to the same total.

Invent and investigate magic shapes of all kinds.
Here are some starters:

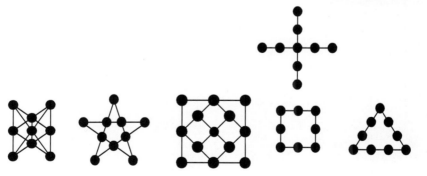

19

36. Rectangle Areas

Some rectangles of area 10 square units have been drawn on squared paper

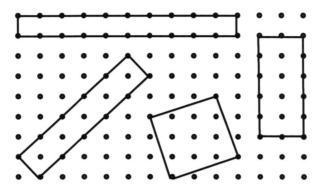

Can you find any more?
What happens if you try other areas?

37. Halving the Board

Here are two ways of cutting a 4 x 4 board into two identical pieces.

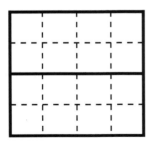 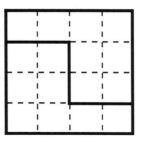

What other ways are there? Investigate other sizes of board.

38. Number Cells

In this row of cells you start with 3 and 4.

3	4			

Then you add 3 and 4 to get 7, then 4 and 7 to get 11, ...

3	4	7	11	18

... but if you are given only the first and last numbers...

8				52

What are the missing numbers?
Try some different first and last numbers. Investigate ways of finding the missing numbers.
Extend to different lengths of cells.

39. Taking Counters

From a pile of counters 2 players alternately take any number, provided that (a) the first player does not take the whole pile and (b) a player does not take more than twice the last number taken. The player taking the last counter wins.
Investigate.

Mathematical Journeys

40. Two-piece Tangrams

Find some possible ways to re-arrange the two
pieces of a square which is cut as shown.

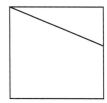

Which of the new shapes that have been generated will tessellate on their own?
Make up some other questions about the two-piece tangram.
What about other simple tangrams you can make using shapes like equilateral triangles or regular hexagons?

41. Lines and Regions

Draw 4 straight lines on a piece of plain paper so that you get the maximum number of crossing points. How many crossing points can you get?
How many inside regions are there? How many outside regions?
Investigate for other numbers of lines.

Mathematical Journeys

42. Patio Tiles

Cover the patio with tiles like this

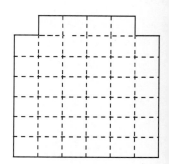

What about this one?

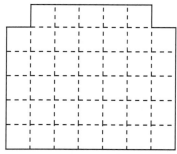

Try other shapes with an area of 40 squares.

43. Near to the Root

"Because 70 is nearer 64 than 81 √70 is nearer 8 than 9"
Test this statement for numbers and their square roots (include some decimals, numbers less than 1 etc.).
For which ranges of numbers is this statement not true?

Mathematical Journeys

44. Calendars

Start with a calendar and investigate the row, column and diagonal patterns.

January 2007	February 2007	March 2007

Mo Tu We Th Fr Sa Su
  1 2 3 4 5 6 7
  8 9 10 11 12 13 14
 15 16 17 18 19 20 21
 22 23 24 25 26 27 28
 29 30 31
	Mo Tu We Th Fr Sa Su
	           1 2 3 4
	  5 6 7 8 9 10 11
	 12 13 14 15 16 17 18
	 19 20 21 22 23 24 25
	 26 27 28
		Mo Tu We Th Fr Sa Su
		           1 2 3 4
		  5 6 7 8 9 10 11
		 12 13 14 15 16 17 18
		 19 20 21 22 23 24 25
		 26 27 28 29 30 31

April 2007	May 2007	June 2007

Mo Tu We Th Fr Sa Su
                    1
  2 3 4 5 6 7 8
  9 10 11 12 13 14 15
 16 17 18 19 20 21 22
 23 24 25 26 27 28 29
 30
	Mo Tu We Th Fr Sa Su
	     1 2 3 4 5 6
	  7 8 9 10 11 12 13
	 14 15 16 17 18 19 20
	 21 22 23 24 25 26 27
	 28 29 30 31
		Mo Tu We Th Fr Sa Su
		              1 2 3
		  4 5 6 7 8 9 10
		 11 12 13 14 15 16 17
		 18 19 20 21 22 23 24
		 25 26 27 28 29 30

July 2007	August 2007	September 2007

Mo Tu We Th Fr Sa Su
                    1
  2 3 4 5 6 7 8
  9 10 11 12 13 14 15
 16 17 18 19 20 21 22
 23 24 25 26 27 28 29
 30 31
	Mo Tu We Th Fr Sa Su
	        1 2 3 4 5
	  6 7 8 9 10 11 12
	 13 14 15 16 17 18 19
	 20 21 22 23 24 25 26
	 27 28 29 30 31
		Mo Tu We Th Fr Sa Su
		                 1 2
		  3 4 5 6 7 8 9
		 10 11 12 13 14 15 16
		 17 18 19 20 21 22 23
		 24 25 26 27 28 29 30

October 2007	November 2007	December 2007

Mo Tu We Th Fr Sa Su
  1 2 3 4 5 6 7
  8 9 10 11 12 13 14
 15 16 17 18 19 20 21
 22 23 24 25 26 27 28
 29 30 31
	Mo Tu We Th Fr Sa Su
	           1 2 3 4
	  5 6 7 8 9 10 11
	 12 13 14 15 16 17 18
	 19 20 21 22 23 24 25
	 26 27 28 29 30
		Mo Tu We Th Fr Sa Su
		                 1 2
		  3 4 5 6 7 8 9
		 10 11 12 13 14 15 16
		 17 18 19 20 21 22 23
		 24 25 26 27 28 29 30
		 31

Look for Friday the 13ths and investigate how many there are in different years.
Which months require six columns? What happens in other years?

45. Quadrant tiles

Draw a circle in the middle of a square. Colour the corners and cut the shape into four equal pieces.

Each of the four tiles now has an identical coloured corner. Arrange the four tiles in a square pattern in any way you like. For example:

Repeat the same pattern, side by side, to make an overall design. The pattern must be the same way round and not reflected or rotated. Investigate how many different overall designs are possible.

Mathematical Journeys

46. Dotty shapes

Make some shapes with no dots inside.

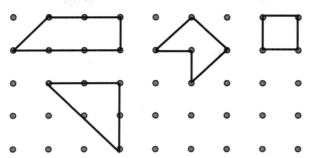

Find the area of each shape and the number of dots on its perimeter. Do the same for shapes with one dot inside, and two dots inside and so on.

47. Polygons within polygons

Within the large equilateral triangle is a regular hexagon. How much of the area is covered by the hexagon?

Find another hexagon which is only half of the area of its surrounding triangle.
Investigate similar problems with equilateral triangles in regular hexagons; with squares in regular octagons and so on.

48. Hiccup numbers

Choose a three-digit number, for example 327, and repeat it, 327327. Divide the numbers by 11; by 13; and by 7 – what happens?
Investigate other 'hiccup' numbers and other situations like this.

25

49. Stamps

You only have 5p and 7p stamps.
It is possible to post a parcel costing 39p (5+5p+5p+5p+5p+5p+5p+7p) but you cannot put the correct amount on a parcel if it costs 23p. What is the biggest parcel that you cannot post?

Make up and investigate problems about stamps and parcels.

50. Maximum Area

What is the biggest area that you can enclose with a perimeter of 24 cm?

51. Breaking Sticks

A stick is broken into three pieces. When can the pieces make a triangle? What is the probability that this can happen?

If the stick is broken into four pieces, what is the probability that they could make a quadrilateral?

52. Moving arrowheads

An 'arrowhead' can be made using counters

Its direction can be changed by moving only five counters

53. Finding triangles

Large equilateral triangles are made up from smaller ones. Investigate the numbers of different sized triangles inside.

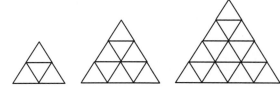

54. Bell ringing

In bell ringing with three bells, there are six different orders in which they can be rung, e.g. (1, 2, 3), (2, 3, 1) etc.
The aim is to produce all six orders before repeating one of them. No bell is allowed to move up or down more than one place from one order to the next, so (1, 2, 3) cannot be followed by (2, 3, 1).
Investigate.

Mathematical Journeys

55. Elephant walk

An elephant, that was very fond of buns, walks through a set of cages each containing one bun.

To get all of the buns the elephant must walk through a minimum of seven cages (there and back).

Try for these sets of cages.

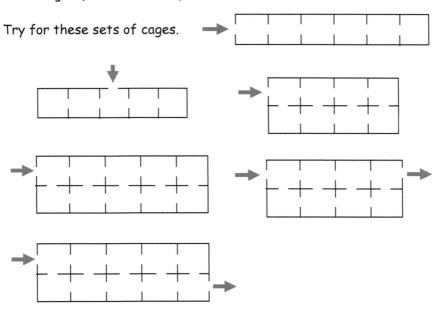

Investigate for different sets of cages with entrances and exits in various places.

Mathematical Journeys

56. Frogs

Try to swap the black and white counters round by either sliding a counter into an empty square or jumping over **one** other counter into another square.
What is the minimum number of moves required?
Investigate for other numbers of counters.

57. Round and Round

Choose any four numbers and place them at the corners of a square

By the middle of side of the square write the difference between the two numbers at the corners of that side.

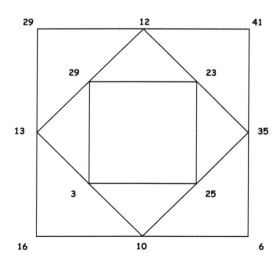

29

Use these numbers for the corners of a new square and repeat the process indefinitely.

Investigate what happens...
Use a triangle instead of a square ... or a pentagon.
Try using quotients instead of differences, perhaps always taking the quotient that gives a value greater than or equal to one.

58. All the Digits

$$12 + 34 + 56 - 78 - 9 = 15$$

$$12 + 345 - 67 - 89 = 201$$

Keeping the digits 1 to nine in order, what numbers can you make?
How will you make exactly 100? Is there only one way to make 100?

59. Quotient

Using a calculator, a three-digit number is divided by another three-digit number. The result is displayed on the calculator as 0.4097807. [Your calculator may show the result differently in the last decimal places.]
What were the two original three-digit numbers?
Can you find a general strategy to discover two original numbers when you are given their quotient as a calculator display?

60. Egyptian Fractions

A unit fraction is a fraction whose numerator is one.

Which fractions can you express as the sum of one or more different unit fractions?

$5/12 = 1/4 + 1/6$

$13/54 = 1/6 + 1/18 + 1/54$

Which fractions can you express in more than one such way?
Any rules?

$19/20 = 1/2 + 1/4 + 1/5 = 1/2 + 1/5 + 1/8 + 1/10 + 1/40$

The ancient Egyptians represented fractions by using different unit fractions, together with the option of using the fraction 2/3.

Investigate the simplest way(s) of writing various fractions the way the Egyptians did

$49/60 = 2/3 + 1/10 + 1/20$

$3/4 = 1/2 + 1/4 = 2/3 + 1/12$

Try adding, subtracting, ... with Egyptian fractions.

61. Frog Hopping

Fergus Frog could never make up his mind.

One day he came to a river. He decided to jump across it, but he only got halfway to the far bank. He then decided to turn round and jump back the way he had come but again only jumped half the distance to the bank. He kept on turning round after each jump, each time only managing to get half the distance he needed to go to get to the bank. Where did he end up?

Try changing the fraction that Fergus jumps from one half to something else and see where Fergus ends up.

Can you make Fergus land wherever you like? What if the fractions varies with each jump?

Invent other jumping rules for Fergus and try them out.

62. Fleas

Seat five people side by side in a straight line. A move is defined as one person changing from a sitting position to a standing position, or from a standing position to a sitting position.

A person can only move when both of the following conditions are satisfied:
1. The person on their immediate left is standing.
2. All the other people on their left are sitting.

The person on the extreme left has no restrictions on their movement.

Can all five people be standing up together?

If so, what is the fewest number of moves in which this can be achieved?

What if the group changes size?

What if the initial state is changed?

63. Garden Path

A rectangular lawn is surrounded by a garden path of constant width.

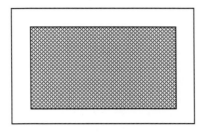

The area of the lawn is exactly equal to the area of the path.

What are the possible values of the length and breadth of the lawn, and of the width of the path, if these are whole numbers?

Extend this idea to three dimensions.

Mathematical Journeys

64. Super-dot Polygons

Investigate polygons with area 8, drawn on squared paper according to the following rules:

1. The vertices of the polygon must lie on the grids points (i.e. at the intersections of the lines of the squared paper.
2. The sides of the polygon must only cut the grid lines at grid points (i.e. they must be at an angle of 45° to the grid lines).

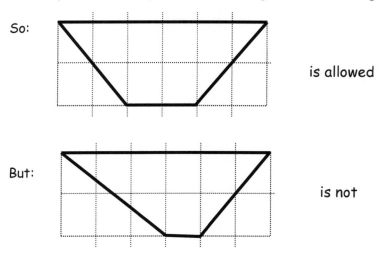

So: is allowed

But: is not

What is the maximum number of sides you can have with area 8?
What is the minimum number of sides?
Try other areas.

35

Mathematical Journeys

65. The Tethered Goat

A goat is tethered to a corner of a hut in the middle of a large field of grass. If the hut is 4 metres by 6 metres and the length of the tether is 9 metres, what area of grass can the goat graze on?
What if the tether is 12 metres long?

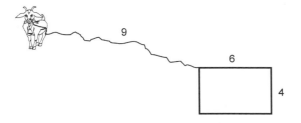

Investigate
- for different tethers;
- for different sizes of hut;
- for more than one goat.

What about non-rectangular huts? Think about circular huts.